"He took to writing poetry and visiting the elves; and though many shook their heads and touched their foreheads and said 'Poor old Baggins!' and though few believed any of his tales, he remained very happy to the end of his days, and those were extraordinarily long."

CLASSIC AUTHORS SERIES

J.R.R. TOLKIEN
Man of Fantasy

———————— • ————————

By Russell Shorto

FOREWORD BY G.B. TENNYSON, PH.D.

THE KIPLING PRESS · NEW YORK

Copyright © 1988 by Russell Shorto
Cover illustration copyright © 1988 by Mark Summers
Illustrations copyright © 1988 by Bill Negron
Photo credits: Pp. 12, 16, 31 courtesy of Culver Pictures;
pp. 26, 36 courtesy of Historical Pictures Service, Chicago; pp. ii, 22, 42
courtesy of AP/Wide World Photos; p. viii courtesy of Ewing Galloway;
p. 6 courtesy of British Tourist Authority.
The endpaper map is a detail of the northwest environs
of London, England.

Printed in the United States
ISBN 0-943718-07-4

The Kipling Press
First Edition

FOREWORD

leading British newspaper recently named *The Hobbit*, by J.R.R. Tolkien, one of the top 100 books all students should read before they graduate high school. Were he alive today, Tolkien might be surprised to see one of his books grouped with the world's great literature—especially one he wrote as a story for his children. But in just fifty years' time, Tolkien's story has become a world classic listed with the Bible, the *Iliad*, *Moby Dick* and Shakespeare's plays.

However, few of Tolkien's readers learned of his work from lists of required reading; most were introduced to his books by friends who had read them. The popularity of Tolkien's tales of dwarves, elves, wizards and ancient adventure is one of the great success stories in literature. Many are surprised to find that the author of these tales of high adventure lived a quiet life as an Oxford University professor.

Born in South Africa in 1892, Tolkien embarked on his longest journey at the age of three, when his English parents decided to return to their homeland. Tolkien's mother brought him and his brother to England alone. His father was supposed to join them later on, but he died before he got the chance. Once in England, Tolkien never saw his father or South Africa again.

Leaving behind the heat and dust of the African veldt, Tolkien grew up around Birmingham, England. He studied at Oxford, fought in France in the First World War, and then settled down to a teaching career. It wasn't long before he returned to Oxford as a professor of Anglo-Saxon (the earliest form of the English language). He stayed at Oxford for the rest of his life, except for a few years of retirement at Bournemouth on the southern coast of England. When his wife died there in 1971, Tolkien once again returned to Oxford, where he lived until his death just two years later.

Since he lived such a quiet life, Tolkien relied more on his imagination than personal experience in writing his stories. Imagination is the key to understanding Tolkien's fiction. His stories offer places of wonder, beauty and valor that ask the reader to use his or her imagination to experience life in worlds that never were. But those worlds are so vivid and convincing that many readers come to believe in them the way that people once believed in myth and legend. Tolkien was so good at making his stories and their settings seem real that his tales have inspired clubs and societies that study the world of Middle-Earth in which Tolkien's hobbits lived.

Although *The Hobbit* began as a story for his children, Tolkien claimed the "the tale grew in the telling." It grew slowly, though, partly because Tolkien had his full share of formal university duties to perform.

However, Tolkien's interest in language and language development (known as the study of philology) shaped his fiction. It is said that Tolkien wrote *The Lord of the Rings* and *The Silmarillion* in order to work out the details of the elfish language he had invented for *The Hobbit*.

The work of Tolkien and some of his associates at Oxford returned the concepts of myth and fantasy to modern literature. Tolkien and his colleagues formed a group known as the Coalbiters (also known as the Oxford Inklings), which included other noted writers of fantasy such as C.S. Lewis and Charles Williams. During their social meetings in the 1930s, Tolkien first read parts of *The Hobbit* to the Coalbiters, and later during World War II, he treated them to passages from *The Lord of the Rings*.

Although his work was respected by his peers, it took two women students who had studied with Tolkien to finally persuade him to publish *The Hobbit*. It took him another seventeen years to bring out *The Lord of the Rings*; by then he already had a dedicated audience. A much larger audience was yet to grow, especially in the United States.

Now that Tolkien's tales are classics, young readers may fear they are unqualified to look into the complex realm he built in his books. Nothing could be further from the truth. Remember that the stories were originally written for Tolkien's children. Tolkien's friend, C.S. Lewis, once said that you had to be either very young or well along in years to enjoy such "fairy stories." It seems safe to say, then, that the only qualifications needed for the reading of J.R.R. Tolkien's magical tales are to be young at heart and full of imagination.

— G.B. Tennyson
University of California, Los Angeles
March 22, 1988

Oxford University

"IN A HOLE IN THE GROUND..."

"... one morning long ago in the quiet of the world, when there was less noise and more green ..."

J R.R. Tolkien, professor of English at Oxford University, sighed as he sat looking at the high stack of examination booklets on his desk. It was summertime and the smell of freshly cut grass blew in on the mild breeze. The last thing he felt like doing was reading exams written by dozens and dozens of youths who hoped to gain admission to Oxford. But he was a man with a growing family—he and his wife, Edith, had three boys, and another child was on the way—and the salary of a professor was not enough to make ends meet. Tolkien had to earn extra income by grading entrance exams during the summer.

He picked one up off the top and began reading. Then he stopped, sighed again, and looked longingly out the window. There, amid ancient, gnarled trees, sat the stately buildings of the university. Tolkien loved Oxford because he loved all things that were old and traditional. His specialty was medieval languages—the dead languages spoken in England and northern Europe in the Middle Ages. He loved the old medieval legends of chivalrous knights who lived in rugged castles and rode their armor-plated horses off in search of adventure. Oxford, with its ancient college buildings and greenery, was one of the few places where Britain's legendary past still seemed to live.

But even here the rapid changes of the past several years were altering life. The year was 1928. It had been ten years since World War I (which was then called the Great War) ended. That first modern War—the first war in which airplanes, machine guns, cars and tanks were used—brought England rushing into the twentieth century. Following it, telephone lines were strung up, new roads laid, and factories built to mass-produce everything from cars to safety pins.

 ven at Oxford, Tolkien could feel the changing times. From his office he could see ancient, moss-covered buildings surrounded by lovely green lawns, but he could also hear the buzz of motorcars—a horrible sound which infuriated him. Brash modern houses were being built in the town, and factories on the outskirts. The students now were ruder and less serious than he and his friends had been in their day. The war had changed all of these things.

It had also changed Tolkien. He was still the slim, long-faced, elegant man who had gone off to fight for his country. But six months in the muddy, corpse-riddled trenches of Europe, shivering with cold, with the blasting of bombs echoing in his ears and the threat of death always near, had changed the young man as it had changed everyone else who had lived through the war. Ronald, as his good friends called him, did not come out of the war with the wild spirit of recklessness that so many others had. Instead, he became more quiet, and dove more deeply into his studies of medieval languages. The present day, and the strange, industrial future that seemed to lie ahead, saddened him.

Now, as he sat correcting exams, he found himself daydreaming, as he often did, of simpler times, of a place where the problems of modern life did not exist. He turned the page of the exam booklet he was reading and found it blank. Suddenly, without even thinking of what he was doing, he picked up his pen and wrote a sentence on the page:

"In a hole in the ground there lived a hobbit."

He frowned as he looked at what he had written. This sentence had nothing to do with the exam. Why did he write it? And what, he asked himself, was a hobbit? What kind of creature was it? What kind of world did it live in?

One thing was certain: whatever a hobbit was, it did not live in the real world, but in one that existed somewhere in Tolkien's mind. It was a fantasy place, where life was simpler than in England of the 1920s. Tolkien was already known in his family as a great storyteller. One of his delights was inventing stories of fantasy kingdoms and legendary heroes to tell to his three boys at bedtime. He never wrote these down, but this time, he decided, he would. Though Tolkien had no idea yet what this world of hobbits was like, he knew he had to find out. He would dive into it.

So then, what exactly is a hobbit? Hobbits, Tolkien discovered when he had thought long enough, are creatures somewhat like people, except that they are smaller, tend to have potbellies, and don't wear shoes because their feet have leathery soles and furry tops. He wrote that they "have long clever brown fingers, good-natured faces, and laugh deep fruity laughs (especially after dinner, which they have twice a day when they can get it.)"

Hobbits are simple, friendly, honest creatures who live in nice, clean holes in the sides of hills. They keep their homes tidy. They like to smoke pipes and eat lots of food. They live in a quiet, peaceful land of gardens, meadows and country roads which Tolkien called the Shire. Tolkien wrote of it as "a wild, respectable country inhabited by decent folk, with good roads, an inn or two, and now and then a dwarf or farmer ambling by on business."

Creating the story of *The Hobbit* gave Tolkien much pleasure. It was a pleasant little world to imagine. But Tolkien soon realized that a peaceful, pleasant world does not make for a good story. For a good tale, one needs adventure. So he made his hobbit, whom he named Bilbo Baggins, go on an adventure with a party of dwarfs and a wizard named Gandalf. And since life in the Shire was always peaceful (and all the hobbits there hate adventures more than anything else), the party had to leave it to have their adventure. They journeyed far through strange lands, and Bilbo Baggins learned how exciting and terrifying and large the world was.

Tolkien worked on the tale on and off for several years, and every time he figured out a new adventure he would gather his sons (and his daughter, when she was old enough) and tell it to them. It was, as he later said, just a story to amuse himself and his children. He never intended to publish it. And he certainly never would have thought, as he sat with his stack of exams on that summer morning in 1928, that someday he would become known as the greatest of fantasy writers, or that his books *The Hobbit* and *The Lord of the Rings* would become as popular as *Alice in Wonderland*.

It would all start with scribbling a sentence in an exam booklet. But although the Shire, the peaceful land of the hobbits, was a fantasy land, it was not created out of thin air. Every writer takes events from his life and molds them into his stories. The Shire was in fact a kind of fanciful dreamland which Tolkien constructed out of his memories of early childhood.

Those were memories of a different England, of a simpler life in a simpler place that is hard for us, in our modern world, to imagine. It was almost a fairy-tale land.

Traditional house in the West Midlands

INVENTING LANGUAGES

"The world was young, the mountains green."

A row of vine-covered, thatch-roofed cottages surrounded by meadows of flowers that sparkled in the sun and bobbed in the wind—this was Ronald Tolkien's boyhood home, the village of Sarehole in the West Midlands of England. There were cool green woods to explore, and on the edge of the village an old stone mill sat astride a lazy stream. Inside, two bearded millers ground corn day in and day out. Ronald and his younger brother Hilary liked to sneak up to the mill and watch as the great big water wheel cranked round and round.

Beside the mill was a placid little pond with swans floating elegantly across its surface. The Tolkien brothers liked to come here and swim on hot summer days while the crickets in the surrounding meadow made a buzzing racket and the sun shone down. But they had to be absolutely quiet because the old miller and his son didn't like little boys snooping about, and if they spotted them in the water the son would sneak up to the bank and steal their socks and shoes. This danger made swimming in the pond all the more fun.

The brothers also liked to hike over the hill to the next village. On the way they would pass an occasional farmer riding his horse-drawn wagon. (The motor car had not even been invented yet.) Once at the village, they would buy candy from a crooked little old woman who had no teeth. When they thanked her, she would cackle and pat their heads.

As an adult, Tolkien always looked back fondly on this happy place of his childhood. Beyond the village were woods that had lain untouched since the days of King Arthur. Thinking back on it, it was sometimes hard for Tolkien to believe that it had really existed. It seemed impossible that the world could change so much in the space of a few decades.

His impressions of the village were so sharp because he was not born in the village of Sarehole, but arrived when he was young and when his mind was alert and impressionable. His first home could not have been more different. He was not born in England at all, but in Africa (of all places), in a place called the Orange Free State, which today is one of the four states in the nation of South Africa.

Arthur Tolkien, Ronald's father, had been a bank manager in England. He was given the opportunity to move to the Orange Free State, where he would have an important job as manager of the Bank of Africa. Not long after he arrived, he sent for his pretty young fiancée, Mabel. After the long sea voyage, she joined him and the two were married in 1891. The next year, Mabel gave birth to their first son, John Ronald Reuel Tolkien. He would become known as J.R.R. Tolkien, but to his friends and family he would be Ronald.

Two years later, the Tolkiens had another son, whom they named Hilary. The two boys were both weak and sickly, and Mabel was anxious to get them out of the hot climate of South Africa. When Ronald was three and Hilary was just a baby in his mother's arms, she decided to go back to England. Arthur would stay for a short while to finish his business, and would then follow.

Even though Ronald was only three years old when he left Africa, strong images of his early life there stayed with him. He remembered it as "a hot parched country," and once wrote: "My first Christmas memory is of blazing sun, drawn curtains and a drooping eucalyptus." Since there were no pine trees in their African home, the Tolkiens had used a native eucalyptus as a Christmas tree.

Also, there were events in Africa that later would become part of the fantasy stories Tolkien would weave. As a boy, Ronald was only allowed to play outside in the early morning and the evening, for during the long midday the heat was too intense. Once when he was playing in the family's garden, he found an interesting object and picked it up. It was a tarantula, a spider with a deadly venom, and it promptly bit him. Ronald dropped it and ran screaming to his nurse, who acted quickly and sucked out the poison.

The image of spiders as fearful creatures stayed with him, and found its way into his tales. In *The Hobbit*, Bilbo Baggins and his dwarf friends encounter an army of huge spiders who live in trees. And in *The Lord of the Rings* the two hobbit heroes encounter a huge and terrifying old spider who wants very much to wrap them in her web and eat them. This is how Tolkien described her:

> Most like a spider she was, but huger than the great hunting beasts, and more terrible than they because of the evil purpose in her remorseless eyes. . . . Great horns she had, and behind her short stalk-like neck was her huge swollen body, a vast bloated bag, swaying and sagging between her legs. . . . As soon as she had squeezed her soft squelching body and its folded limbs out of the upper exit from her lair, she moved with a horrible speed, now running on her creaking legs, now making a sudden bound.

So it would seem that Tolkien's first encounter with a spider left him with a bad feeling about them!

At the age of three Ronald left Africa with his mother and brother, and moved to England and the sleepy village of Sarehole. The boy was very impressionable. Everything about his new home, from the soft, green countryside to the chilly winter days spent by a crackling fire, thrilled him. Somehow he sensed that he belonged here, in the lovely English countryside. All his life that feeling would remain.

When, as a young university professor, J.R.R. Tolkien would pick up a pen and scrawl the first sentence of *The Hobbit* into a student's exam booklet, he would transform his pleasant memories of his childhood village of Sarehole into the Shire, the land of the hobbits. And the people of Sarehole—good, simple, hard-working farmers and jolly shopkeepers—would become the model for the hobbits themselves. "I took the idea of the hobbits from the village people and children," he once said. Their simple, honest, homespun ways made him feel warm and comfortable. The life of a small village without the bother of motor-cars and telephones was, to him, the perfect life.

After leaving Africa, Ronald was never to see his father again. Less than a year later Arthur Tolkien contracted rheumatic fever and died. The only memories Ronald was to have of his father were dim ones of a thin man with a large, drooping moustache, standing tall in the hot sun.

Mabel Tolkien took charge of the sons. As they grew she became not only their mother but their teacher as well. When Ronald was only five she began teaching him Latin and French. The boy's first few lessons were a marvelous experience. A whole new world was opening up for him, a wondrous world of letters and sounds and meanings. The idea that there were different languages—different ways to say things about the world around him—thrilled him. He delighted in discovering the different kinds of sounds each language used, and he never tired of learning new words and expressions.

By the time he was nine, Ronald could read and write Latin, Greek and French. And the mystery of languages continued to captivate him. He set about very carefully working out a language of his own, one that used nouns and verbs and other parts of speech just as the other languages he had learned, but one in which all the words were ones he himself had made up. Sitting in a big, overstuffed chair in the family parlor, Ronald would carefully write messages and letters to himself in his secret, private language. Later he would read them, and would shiver with delight as he understood the meaning.

He also did plenty of reading. A few decades before, an English mathematician named Charles Lutwidge Dodgson had taken the children of a friend boating, and one of them, a girl named Alice Liddel, had asked him to write a story about her. Dodgson's story, which he published under the pen name Lewis Carroll, was called *Alice's Adventures in Wonderland.* By Tolkien's time it was already a classic. Ronald read it eagerly and was introduced to a world of fantasy. He later read, and liked even more, the stories of King Arthur and the Knights of the Round Table. Here were tales of adventure and daring out of England's glorious past. Images of that legendary past flooded Ronald's young mind. He wished above all things to be able to go back to that time when the clang of armor sounded as

Lewis Carroll

knights on horseback jousted in cold morning air.

All in all, Ronald Tolkien, and his younger brother Hilary, had a pleasant, cozy childhood, taught and cared for by their loving mother in the charming cottage in the village of Sarehole. Then, quite suddenly, it all came to an end. In 1904 Mabel Tolkien learned that she had diabetes, a disease which at that time could not be controlled. The little family moved into a cottage with a postman and his wife so that the wife could help care for Mabel and cook for the boys. For most of the year this was the situation, and Mabel's condition even started to improve. Then, in November, she suddenly fell desperately ill and, as her two young boys sat together nervously fidgeting while adults hovered over their mother's bed, she died.

The months following their mother's death was a time of confusion and sadness for the two boys. They were old enough to understand that she would never again be with them, but they were still children and completely dependent on her. They would be cared for somehow, of course. But Ronald Tolkien didn't seem to care. The past, and the lovely time spent with his mother, was gone. Though he was only twelve, he now realized something that it takes most people all their lives to appreciate: that nothing in life lasts forever.

One of the things Mabel Tolkien had left her sons was a strong religious belief. She had been raised in the predominant Protestant sect in England, the Church of England, but had become a Roman Catholic as an adult. When she died, she left her two boys in the care of her priest, Father Francis Morgan.

Father Morgan was a tall, imposing man, but he had a kindly smile and he truly cared for the two boys. Although they never felt for him the love one feels for a parent, they quickly became attached to him. After their mother's death they were moved into a home for orphans in Birmingham and began attending school. The boys were often struck with sadness at the death of their mother and the strange new surroundings, but Father Morgan visited them often and took them on trips into the countryside. Once they went with him on a long journey to Wales, the rugged land in the west of Britain. There Ronald first encountered the Welsh language. It delighted him that an ancient language was still alive in the lilting voices of train conductors

and written on roadsigns. He determined to learn this wonderful old tongue. His love of languages was continuing, but he had by now realized that the languages most students learned—Latin, Greek and modern European languages—didn't interest him as much as the dead languages of Northern Europe. Here, he secretly decided, would be his own special subject.

When Ronald was sixteen and Hilary was fourteen, they were moved to another house, this one owned by a wine seller named Faulkner and his blustery wife. The old couple took in boarders in order to make a few extra shillings, and were happy to have the two boys. They already had one orphan living in the house, a girl named Edith Bratt.

Edith was a small, pretty girl whose mother had died several years before, leaving her with nowhere to go. Her distant relatives had arranged a place for her in the boardinghouse. She was nineteen and so almost three years older than Ronald. But the two quickly became friends, and then, gradually, they fell in love.

Edith was an excellent piano player, and Ronald loved to sit in the parlor listening to her play. She in turn was captivated by his intelligence and skill with languages. The two would sit together snickering about fussy old Mrs. Faulkner, who always seemed to be complaining about the amount of noise her young boarders made.

Edith was naturally shy, but with Ronald she was open and friendly. She had soft, shining eyes and a pretty figure. Ronald, at sixteen, looked older. He had a long, thin face, serious eyes, and careful manners. The two young lovers could not, of course, let the household know of their feelings for each other. Instead, they met secretly. Eventually, Mrs. Faulkner found out about their feelings and told their guardians. Edith's aunt and uncle immediately removed her from the house and forbade her to see or to write to Ronald Tolkien ever again.

Ronald was saddened by this separation, but he determined that it would not be forever. He would be an adult soon, and then he would formally announce his intention of marrying Edith.

For now, though, his attention shifted. In 1910 he won a scholarship to attend Oxford University, and his life changed completely. Childhood was behind him. A new world lay ahead.

Boat racing near Oxford

THE END OF THE GOOD OLD DAYS

"Fell deeds awake: fire and slaughter! spear shall be shaken, shield be splintered, a sword-day, a red day, ere the sun rises!"

Oxford was everything that Ronald Tolkien could have hoped for. The buildings of the separate colleges of the university were ancient, some dating back to Tolkien's beloved Middle Ages. Oxford University was the oldest in England, and one of the oldest in the world. Medieval knights and barons had sent their sons to be educated there six hundred years before Tolkien's time. Walking through its shady groves and alongside the stone build-

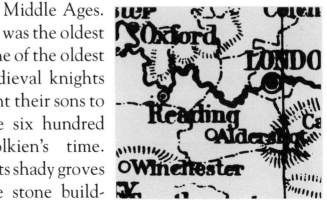

ings, Ronald Tolkien would close his eyes and the swarthy knights and squires of the distant past would seem to jump to life.

Tolkien attended Exeter College. Oxford and Cambridge, England's two most prestigious universities, are both divided into a number of colleges. These are simply old, tradition-laden halls where the students live and have their meals. Every student at Oxford was officially a member of one of the colleges. Some of the colleges were known for their stately rooms, some for the great men who had once lived there, some for the fine food they served. Exeter was known for the excellence of its students.

Ronald Tolkien was a popular figure at college. He was a fine sportsman and liked to play cricket, rugby and tennis. He was a good joke-teller. When not studying, he and several friends liked to make the rounds of the local pubs, which had names like the Royal Oak and the King's Arms. There, wearing their long black student's robes (they were required to wear their robes at all times), they would sit drinking pints of ale and discussing teachers, books, and girls.

Ronald studied languages, of course. But instead of Latin and Greek, which most of his friends chose to study, he preferred Medieval Finnish, Old Norse and Anglo-Saxon. These languages, spoken by peoples of Northern Europe in the darkest Middle Ages, seemed as strange to Tolkien's friends as they do to most people now. But Ronald had learned a special secret about them—their myths. He was eager to study the languages not to be able to speak them (for, after all, the last living speakers had died centuries before), but to read them. For the myths written in these languages—epic tales of questing heroes, of good and evil—seemed to Ronald Tolkien to be the most exciting tales ever told.

One of his teachers, W. A. Craigie, was an expert in philology,

the study of how languages are created and changed over time. Tolkien mentioned once to Craigie that he had played at inventing his own languages in the past, just for the fun of it. Craigie begged his student to show him his private language. Tolkien did, and soon the two were examining it in detail and were deep in conversation about how it might be made more complete and realistic. They were not simply playing a game, but were interested in how languages are formed. Just as a scientist might try to grow a new kind of plant in order to understand how plants work, Tolkien and Craigie set about trying to "grow" a language.

Tolkien loved everything about university life. Unfortunately for him, though, things were not to last. The quiet life of the Oxford scholars was about to come to a halt. Soon there were to be no more groups of students strolling peacefully under the trees in their black gowns. Oxford, England, and Ronald Tolkien were about to be changed forever. Rumors had started to drift over the crusty walls of the university from the outside world: rumors of war.

The nations of Europe were falling into two parties that were growing more and more angry with one another. Over the past few years there had been dozens of small-scale battles and invasions in Eastern Europe and North Africa. Smaller nations like Serbia, Albania and Montenegro quarreled with one another and with the great empire of Austria-Hungary. Soon Italy and Greece became involved. Then Russia and Germany began their own dispute.

In 1914, while Ronald Tolkien was still spending his days as a happy scholar at Oxford, a Serbian assassin shot and killed the Austrian archduke. All the tensions that had been building up in Europe erupted. Like a series of firecrackers, war exploded across Europe. Austria-Hungary declared war on Serbia. Russia, alarmed, mobilized its troops. Germany, seeing Russian troops amassing, declared war on Russia. France, Italy, Greece and even Japan entered the war.

Then, in August of 1914, Germany invaded Belgium. This news swept across England like a dark, ominous cloud, for England was committed to protecting Belgium. Paper boys ran through the streets screaming out the headlines. Shopkeepers walked out into the street scratching their heads. Policemen and passersby heard the news and their hearts sank. Until now England had hoped to avoid the war. But this invasion decided the matter once and for all. England would have to fight.

At Oxford, student life suddenly ground to a halt as the scholars abandoned their studies and enlisted in the army. Oxford's colleges were transformed into army barracks, and the fine college lawns became drill camps. Ronald Tolkien remained a student long enough to finish his final year and earn his degree; then he, too, signed up.

He spent the next several months at the army's training grounds in Bedford. He was granted the rank of second lieutenant and spent his days drilling platoons of new recruits, marching them up and down the parade ground in smart lines. He had brought a few volumes of Norse myths with him, and when he had a spare moment he dipped into them. But there was little time for that. His duties took up nearly all his waking hours. One duty that he quickly learned to enjoy was signalling: the sending of communications by flags, lamps, or Morse code. He became expert at this, which is not surprising since it is really a form of language, and he was ever fascinated by languages.

Early in 1916, Tolkien's battalion got the word to get ready to head to France for war. As the fateful day approached, Tolkien's thoughts turned more and more to the idea of how much the world had changed. Only a few months ago he had been a happy student. Now he was about to go off into battle, where he would very probably be killed. News from the front reported horrors untold in human history. There were single battles in which more than 100,000 men were killed.

What kind of new world was this he was living in? What kind of governments could put up with such killing? Ronald Tolkien felt a deep sadness as though something were about to die, but he wasn't sure whether it was him, or the old traditions of England.

Then, suddenly, his mood swung around. The gloom fled from his mind and in its place a bright love of life burst forth. He suddenly felt he had to grasp at something—to hold on to life. He and Edith had continued to communicate through the past few years despite her aunt and uncle's objections, and they had promised to marry. Now, with the time to embark for battle approaching, he journeyed to Warwickshire. Edith was at the station to meet him. Surrounded by platoons of young men in army dress headed for the front, the young couple embraced on the train platform and tears sprang up in both of their eyes. Neither

knew what would happen over the next weeks and months, whether Ronald would live or die. But both wanted to grab on to the present and to express their love.

They were married on March 22, 1916. One week later, Ronald Tolkien left England for war.

Bombs exploding on the distant plains lighted up the night landscape. Their light flickered on the grimy, sweaty faces of men and boys huddled like worms in a long, deep trench dug in the muddy earth. Coughing, crying and moaning wafted through the air from all sides. Horrible, putrid smells surrounded the trenches. A few hundred yards away lay the trenches of the enemy. Lieutenant Tolkien and his men, like all the British soldiers in the trenches, were tired, numb and frightened. Nevertheless, they slowly shouldered their heavy equipment and prepared, on the order, to leap out of the trenches and dash for the enemy lines.

The bombing by the British had gone on for days. The British generals thought this would weaken the Germans so that troops could march on them. But the German leaders realized that such an extensive bombing raid would be followed by an advance, and they were ready.

On the signal to attack, a vast swarm of British soldiers crawled out of their trenches and, bogged down by sixty-six pound equipment packs, trudged off. . .to their death. The Germans were ready with one of the war's deadliest new weapons: machine guns. When the British had gotten close enough, they opened fire. The powerful guns tore through the line of soldiers, ripping them apart. The battle was a complete disaster. Of the sixty thousand British soldiers who advanced on the enemy, only ten thousand survived.

Ronald Tolkien was among them. At the end of the advance, covered with mud and nearly bowed over under the weight of his pack, he stood and felt his arms, legs and face to convince himself that all his parts were really intact. He couldn't believe his fortune. He had been certain that he would meet his end here on the muddy, shell-pocked plain of the Somme River. Unbelievably, he wasn't even injured.

But the Battle of the Somme wasn't the end of the war for Lieutenant Tolkien. The soldiers now had to hold their front-line position against attack. This phase was slow and agonizing work. Week upon week the weary men lived in their trenches, forever filthy, with blood-caked injuries that were never tended properly. Occasionally the Germans would unleash their latest weapon—great clouds of poisonous chlorine gas—and there would be a mad scramble as the men looked for their gas masks and hurriedly put them on before the choking gas overwhelmed them. And as the months wore on, the weather turned colder and a numbing chill set into skin and bones.

Even more dreaded than the enemy was disease. Sitting for weeks in their own filth, soaking wet night and day, the men came down with one disease after another. In October, Tolkien

fell into a delirium. His body shook, his head spun, he felt on fire though he was lying in cold muddy water. Doctors diagnosed it as "trench fever," the most dreaded disease of the war, which was transmitted by the horrible lice that infested the bodies of soldiers in the trenches.

Tolkien was removed to a hospital, and, as soon as he was well enough, was taken back to England to recuperate. There, slowly, he came to himself again. The long, dreary, soaking months in the trenches had worn his mind into a mush. Now for the first time since the Battle of the Somme he was able to think clearly.

But thinking pained him. After all, what was there to think about but the war? True, he had survived, and he would not be sent back into active duty. He wasn't thinking about himself, though, but about Europe. What was happening in the world? Had everyone gone insane? In all of history, there had never been a war of such hideous brutality and such terrifyingly large-scale slaughter. Modern technology, which Tolkien had always distrusted, had made it possible. People nowadays were forever praising science and the wonders it would bring. But as far as he could see it had brought only destruction. Thanks to science, there were frighteningly deadly machine guns, airplanes that could attack with blinding speed, and poisonous gases that tortured, maimed and killed masses of men.

Tolkien had never been a lover of war, but at least in the old days a war could be conducted on a personal level. If you wanted to fight some in the Middle Ages, it was only the two of you, facing one another on foot or on horseback. It was a personal battle, between two individuals who could look in one another's eyes. There was something honest about that kind of combat. Now warfare had grown on to a mass scale. With bombs, airplanes and gases, one could destroy hundreds or thousands of men without even seeing them, without looking them in the eyes. It was all too horrible for Tolkien to think about. He couldn't believe the mass insanity that seemed to have overtaken the world.

He turned his attention, when he was well enough, to writing. Slowly at first, then with growing interest, he sketched the outlines of a different world, a fantasy world. He wasn't writing a story exactly. It was more like a collection of myths. It was, in fact, the mythology of the world of his private language. He called his language Elvish, and he set about creating a world in which the elves who spoke Elvish lived. He imagined a great history for the elves, a history of kingdoms and princes, common folk, nations and villages.

It was a vast work: so vast, in fact, that he would never finish it, though he would work on it all his life. It would be published, finally, after his death, and would be called *The Silmarillion*. And although it was not a story in itself, it would provide the background for the fictional world that he was about to create.

The whole world was changing, and J. R. R. Tolkien, who didn't like it one bit, dealt with it in the only way he was able to. He abandoned the ugly new world, and made one of his own.

World War I Armistice Celebration in England

"...THERE LIVED A HOBBIT"

"'We are plain quiet folk and have no use for adventures.
Nasty disturbing uncomfortable things! Make you late for dinner!
I can't think of what anybody sees in them,' said our Mr. Baggins . . .'"

The Union Jack, the English flag, flapped briskly in the breeze. Behind it, all down the long, stately street to Westminster Abbey and the Houses of Parliament, marched the platoons and divisions of Britain's army. The crowds that jammed the sidewalks cheered as each group passed. Flags waved, confetti tumbled down, the whole city of London was alive with happiness. The Great War was over and the Allies—England, France, Russia and the United States—had won.

Fifty miles away at Oxford University there were celebrations too. Professors and students

joined in cheering in the victory. "The War to End all Wars" was over at last, and the university could now get back to its proper business.

J.R.R. Tolkien was back in Oxford, but no longer as a student. He had gone in hopes of getting a professorship, but found that there were no positions open. He got lucky, though, when he went to see his old friend, Professor Craigie. The older English professors were hard at work on a grand new edition of the *Oxford English Dictionary*, the greatest dictionary of the English language, and, at Craigie's urging, they asked young Tolkien to assist them. His knowledge of obscure languages would be invaluable in helping to trace the meanings of various English words back through time.

Tolkien dove into this task with delight. Weeks would go by when it seemed to Edith that her husband was not living in the present at all, but wading through ancient conquests of England by Northern European tribes like the Angles and Saxons, tracing modern English words back to their roots in the languages of these tribes.

These were happy years for Ronald and Edith Tolkien. Ronald's income was small, but that didn't matter. They felt lucky being together at all, for all but one of Ronald's Oxford chums had been killed in the war. If the Tolkiens' own lives were not enough to be happy about, they now had a son, John. The little family lived in a comfortable home that was just large enough for Edith to have a piano. For Ronald it was just a short walk to the offices of the dictionary staff.

He had joined the mammoth project of the *Oxford English Dictionary* near its end. It had been started forty years before, and by now the busy compilers and checkers had proceeded—alphabetically, of course—most of the way through the words of the language. The section from W to Z was still to be done, and it was this that Tolkien helped on.

Eventually, the work slowed, and Tolkien, in need of money to support his growing family, got an offer to be a professor at Leeds University. He took the job, and the family moved north to the city of Leeds. That same year, though, a position opened up at Oxford and it was offered to Tolkien. Overjoyed at the prospect of returning to his beloved Oxford, he accepted, sent a formal letter to the head of the department at Leeds expressing his regret for leaving so suddenly, and, packing his family up once again, headed back to Oxford.

inally his dream had come true; he was an Oxford professor. There were lectures to be given to rooms full of bright-eyed students. (Tolkien liked to think up ways to make the subject of dead languages come alive for his students. Sometimes he would make up crossword puzzles in Anglo-Saxon for them to figure out.) There was also, of course, research to be done on medieval texts. And there were new friends. He made several lasting friendships with other members of the faculty. His closest friend was C.S. Lewis, who was also to become known as a great fantasy writer.

The two men hit it off as soon as they met. They were the two youngest members of the English faculty and Tolkien found, to his delight, that Lewis was a great fan of the Norse myths. Soon after they met they were deep in discussion. The first conversation was continued on their next meeting, and then on the next. They began getting together with other professors who shared some of their interests. This group usually met at a pub, and, although they weren't exactly a club, they had a name for themselves: the Coalbiters.

Lewis and Tolkien spent many cheery evenings with the other Coalbiters. But they enjoyed most going off on long walks in the countryside together, all the while chattering about the ancient myths and legends. They also talked about religion. Both were deeply religious men, and although Tolkien was a Catholic and Lewis a member of the Church of England, they respected one another's views.

Tolkien now had many things to be happy about: his friendship with Lewis, his love for his wife and for his three sons (two more boys, Michael and Christopher, had been born by now), and his position at Oxford. But there was still something gnawing inside him. He loved his work and his surroundings, but he could not ignore the fact that, since the war, life had changed a great deal.

Everyone who lived through World War I was profoundly affected by it. It changed the world—bringing airplanes, factories, and so forth—but it also changed people's minds. Everyone had the feeling that the simple life—the life that humans had lived ever since there were humans and before science and machines began to change things—was gone forever. And no one quite understood what the future would hold.

While everyone had been affected by the war, people's reactions were different. Some were angry and used the changes of the war to bring about even more changes. In Russia, there was revolution. In England, coal miners and other workers went on massive strikes and insisted on better working conditions. Never before had such large-scale demands been made.

Other people were confused by the new age that was upon them. They drifted aimlessly. Unable to fit into society, they spent their time at parties and in bars and pubs. They decided that if they couldn't be stable they would at least have fun. Writers like Ernest Hemingway and F. Scott Fitzgerald wrote stories about such lost people searching for happiness. They became known as "the Lost Generation."

But Tolkien did not react like any of these people. He didn't lash out, and he didn't waste his life away in pubs. Instead, he reacted to the new, modern world by turning to fiction. It was at this time that, while grading entrance examinations, he suddenly scribbled the opening sentence to *The Hobbit*: "In a hole in a ground there lived a hobbit." It took him several years to write the book. His office

F. Scott Fitzgerald

in the family house was in the attic, and it was cold in winter and stiflingly hot in summer. He would sit on the edge of an old cot and write in his careful, brittle handwriting in a notebook that he propped up on a desk. As he created the story he wove many things from the Norse myths into it. For example, he did not think up the names of the dwarfs that brought Bilbo Baggins on their adventure. Those names—Fili, Kili, Bofur, Bifur, Bombur, Nori, Dori, Ori, Balin, Dwalin, Oin, Gloin and Thorin—are all from a Norse legend. So, in fact, is the name Tolkien used for the great wizard who leads the party: Gandalf.

When Tolkien finished the story, he passed it around to the

Coalbiters, who found it most amusing, and of course he had been reading parts of it to his children all along. But that, as far as Tolkien was concerned, was the end of it. It was stuck in a drawer, and that was that.

Then one of Tolkien's former students, who had read the story, happened to be talking with another former student, named Susan Dagnell, who now worked for the publishing firm of Allen & Unwin. She told Susan Dagnell that she thought *The Hobbit* would make a wonderful book. Dagnell had a long meeting with Professor Tolkien, and although he shook his head several times during the course of it, she ended up by getting him to give her a copy.

She, in turn, gave the copy to her boss, Sir Stanley Unwin. Sir Stanley was a very learned man, but he didn't consider himself an expert in children's books. (Since Tolkien had written this story for his children, it was decided that it was a children's book.) So, instead of reading it himself, Sir Stanley gave it to an expert: his ten-year-old son, Rayner. The father and son had an agreement: Rayner would read any stories his father gave him, and then write a short report about them. He would get one shilling per book.

This is what Rayner Unwin wrote about *The Hobbit*:

> *Bilbo Baggins was a hobbit who lived in his hobbit-hole and never went for adventures. At last Gandalf the wizard and his dwarves persuaded him to go. He had a very exciting time fighting goblins and wargs. At last they got to the lonely mountain; Smaug, the dragon who guards it is killed and after a terrific battle with the goblins he returned home— rich! This book, with the help of maps, does not need any illustrations. It is good and should appeal to all children between the ages of 5 and 9.*

Young Rayner Unwin obviously liked the book—Sir Stanley could see that. He decided to follow his son's advice and publish *The Hobbit*. He only disagreed with Rayner about illustrations: when the book was published, it contained drawings by Tolkien himself. And Rayner was wrong about the age group the book was written for: it is not just for "children between the ages of 5 and 9," but for all children and adults, too.

J.R.R. Tolkien was surely the most excited man in Oxford one September morning in 1937. He paced back and forth across his living room, fidgeting with coins in his pocket while Edith watched him and shook her head. Finally there was a knock at the door. It was a delivery for Professor Tolkien from the publishing house of Allen & Unwin. Here it was: *The Hobbit*! Tolkien unwrapped his copy of the book and a smile spread across his face as he skimmed through the pages, stopping at the drawings. Edith hugged him, then took the book from him and settled into a chair with it.

The Hobbit pleased its author, and it pleased plenty of other people too. Newspaper reviewers raved over it. *The Times*, London's most prestigious newspaper, called Tolkien "a new star." (This was very kind, but the reviewer was not exactly a stranger: it was none other than C.S. Lewis.) *The Hobbit* was published in the United States soon afterwards, and it quickly received a prize as the best children's book of the year.

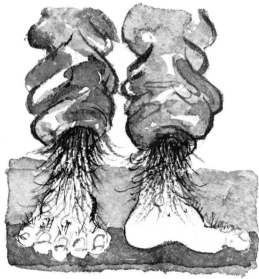

In spite of this, however, the book did not sell all that well. Nevertheless, Tolkien was happy. And Sir Stanley Unwin was too. He recognized that here was a book that would sell steadily year after year, and continue to make money for his firm. He soon met with Professor Tolkien and asked for more stories about hobbits. Tolkien, delighted at the attention, promptly sent his long, windy, unfinished mythology, *The Silmarillion*. It was so long it arrived in several packages. Some of it was typed and other parts written by hand. There were scribbles and coffee stains all over it. Nevertheless, Sir Stanley read through most of it. He quickly saw, however, that this was *not* another story about hobbits. In fact, it wasn't a story at all. He wrote to Tolkien politely rejecting *The Silmarillion* and saying, "I still hope you will be inspired to write another book about the Hobbit."

Tolkien was disappointed that the publisher did not want *The Silmarillion*, but he was hardly surprised. It was, after all, an extremely complicated history of the elf kingdoms, and it was not written as a story. Clearly, people would be much more interested in reading a story than a long, fanciful mythology. Tolkien wrote back to Sir Stanley, saying that he, too, thought the public would like to read more about hobbits. "I promise to give this thought and attention," he wrote. But he admitted that "the construction of elaborate and consistent mythology" in *The Silmarillion* was what most interested him.

He would think about a follow-up to *The Hobbit*, but he had no clear idea what it might be. He promised to give it a try, but, he warned Sir Stanley, "goodness knows what will happen."

He would think about a follow-up to *The Hobbit*, but he had no clear idea what it might be. He promised to give it a try, but, he warned Sir Stanley: "Goodness knows what will happen."

THE LORD OF THE RINGS

"One Ring to rule them all, One Ring to find them,
One Ring to bring them all and in the darkness blind them"

A s Professor Tolkien sat in his Oxford office and tried to think of a way to continue his story about hobbits, events in the outside world were swiftly bringing changes once again. Again there was talk of a great war coming. With horror, Tolkien listened to the talk in pubs of the events taking shape in Europe. If another world war comes, people were saying, it would be far more terrible than the last.

At the end of the last war, Germany had been the great loser. The victors had imposed harsh conditions on Germany, hoping to ensure that never again would

Adolf Hitler reviewing Nazi troops

a German military power attempt to overwhelm Europe. But the harsh conditions only led to anger among Germans. Over the next two decades, more and more German citizens who were bitter at their treatment joined the ranks of Adolf Hitler's Nazi Party. The Nazis came to power in 1933, while J.R.R. Tolkien was quietly working away on *The Hobbit*. They promised to revive the German military establishment, and to lead Germany to dominance of Europe and of the world.

In 1939, Germany began its attack on Poland. Now the rumors of coming war that had blazed across England proved true. England could not sit back and allow this to happen. England and France both declared war on Germany late in 1939. Soon Italy joined the Germans and, as in World War I, a host of other countries fell in line behind one side or the other.

But the war was on a much larger scale than the last. Here the fighting raged not only in Europe but in North Africa, on tiny islands in the South Pacific, and in the jungles of the Philippines.

Sitting in pubs at Oxford with C. S. Lewis, Tolkien pondered the terrifying new war that was raging. He was not a political man; nevertheless, he could not ignore the war. In pubs, on street corners, in newspapers, it was the only thing talked about.

It even entered Tolkien's ideas about his new work to follow *The Hobbit*. In *The Hobbit* he had imagined a peaceful little world, and especially a tranquil land where the hobbits lived. That came out of his memories of childhood in the village of Sarehole. His new work, though, would be influenced not by the past, but by the present. It would be a long tale of adventure set in the same fantasy world. But now there would be a darkness hovering over all, just as the darkness of war hovered over Europe. He would build an epic tale of good and evil, of approaching darkness, and, finally, of war.

But how could he connect such a story with *The Hobbit*? What relationship would there be? Sir Stanley definitely said his readers wanted a story about more hobbits. Finally, it hit Tolkien. In *The Hobbit*, Bilbo finds a magical ring that, when he puts it on, makes him invisible. At the end of the story, he returns home and lives happily ever after, but he keeps the ring.

Now Tolkien decided that the ring would be the perfect thing to link the two stories. It would be no ordinary ring, but the ring of the Dark Lord, the terrifying evil wizard whose goal was to rule the world with his dark power. In this way, Tolkien connected the simple tale told in *The Hobbit* with the grand, intricate mythology of *The Silmarillion*. The resulting book, which Tolkien called *The Lord of the Rings*, would be an adventure story featuring hobbits, and it would also use Tolkien's invented mythology.

For several days, Tolkien daydreamed about his plans for the new book. He wanted to include a short poem at the front of the book that would explain the history of the rings—for, he had decided, there should be several "rings of power" in the story, and Bilbo's should be the most powerful. One night while he was taking a bath the whole poem took shape in his mind. He leaped up, dripping wet, ran to get a piece of paper, and wrote the poem:

> *Three Rings for the Elven-kings under the sky,*
> *Seven for the Dwarf-lords in their halls of stone,*
> *Nine for Mortal Men doomed to die,*
> *One for the Dark Lord on his dark throne*
> *In the Land of Mordor where the Shadows lie.*
> *One Ring to rule them all, One Ring to find them,*
> *One Ring to bring them all and in the darkness bind them*
> *In the Land of Mordor where the Shadows lie.*

The actual writing of the story, however, went slowly. The war years were not a good time for creative projects. Tolkien worked on *The Lord of the Rings* for ten years. During that time the war

raged on, and was finally won. In Oxford, changes occurred daily as real estate was bought by developers and the ancient little town began to take on a new atmosphere. The Tolkiens' children were all grown by now: John, their eldest son, who used to listen wide-eyed to his father's made-up tales, was a man of thirty-two by the time the project was finished.

At last, in 1950, Tolkien sent the completed manuscript to the offices of Allen & Unwin. Rayner Unwin was now a grown man and working at the firm. He had been reading parts of the book as Tolkien wrote them, so that Rayner and *The Lord of the Rings* grew up together. He was eager to finally see the finished product.

Pleased and relieved that all his work had not gone for nothing, Tolkien handed it over.

At last, fifteen years after Sir Stanley Unwin suggested that Tolkien write a sequel to *The Hobbit*, Allen & Unwin published *The Lord of the Rings*. It was so long that the publishers split it into three volumes. Tolkien didn't like this idea, but he gave in and submitted titles for the three: *The Fellowship of the Ring*, *The Two Towers*, and *The Return of the King*. The first volume appeared finally in 1954. Allen & Unwin were happy to publish it, but they didn't think it would sell very well, so they only issued 3,500 copies.

And, for a time, they were right in thinking Tolkien's work would not make much money. It received a few fine reviews, but the public did not dash to bookstores to buy it. Slowly, however, the publishers noticed that copies *were* being bought. It was not a best seller, but it was having steady sales. In fact, *The Lord of the Rings* had been discovered on university campuses. Students and professors were reading the long adventure, filled with details of the mythology of the elves, and were fascinated by it. It was not only a fun and exciting story, but, they realized, it was expertly written.

As the decade of the 1950s progressed, the book's sales increased instead of decreasing, as was usual with a new title. Meanwhile, it continued to be reviewed in magazines in England and the United States.

In 1959, J.R.R. Tolkien, now sixty-six years old, retired from his professorship at Oxford. He gave a final lecture to a great assembly of students and professors. He talked not at all about his popular fiction, but about medieval scholarship, which was, after all, his field. He then settled into the happy, quiet life of a retired professor. He and Edith had a nice home. Their children were now all grown and moved away, but, as always, they had each other.

Tolkien's hair had turned grey some time ago, and his eyebrows had gotten bushy. He had also grown a bit plump, but he still had his crisp laugh, and the sparkle in his eyes seemed to grow brighter as he aged.

Sitting together in their living room, thinking back on their life, the Tolkiens had to admit it had been a good one. They had seen a great deal of change in the world—and most of it for the worse, they thought—but they had been lucky in their own lives.

They didn't realize that life was not finished surprising them.

Students protesting Vietnam war

FRODO LIVES

"Let them a journey new begin,
But I at last with weary feet
Will turn towards the lighted inn,
My evening-rest and sleep to meet."

The big change in the Tolkiens' life was to occur far away from their Oxford home—in the United States of America. It was now 1965, and America was in a state of crisis. Across the country, young people had lost faith in their parents' dreams. They no longer saw their country as a land of opportunity, but as a great mass of highways, factories and shops. Industry was poisoning the water and air. The nation was fighting the Vietnam War, which most young people thought was wrong.

It was a time when America's youth were frustrated and confused. They didn't believe in the world of

their parents. They wanted to strike out on their own, to create a better world, one not ruined by wars and machines.

In a sense, this was just the kind of world J.R.R. Tolkien had created decades before. *The Hobbit* and *The Lord of the Rings* were all about a simpler world in which people did not try to destroy nature. Tolkien had never liked the modern world. In America, a whole generation had sprung up that shared his views.

Tolkien's books had sold decently in America, but not outstandingly. They had only been printed in hardcover, which was quite expensive, and the publishers were delaying printing a paperback edition.

But another publisher in the United States, a science fiction publisher called Ace Books, realized that Tolkien's books were perfect for the mood in the country. If they could be published in paperback, with a huge printing of hundreds of thousands of copies, they would be sure to sell out. This is exactly what Ace Books did: they printed a huge number of copies of *The Hobbit* and *The Lord of the Rings*. Instantly they were bought up. Students all over America began reading the books. They became instant classics.

The only problem was Ace Books was not the authorized publisher. They had printed the book without making an arrangement with Allen & Unwin. There was a terrific battle among the publishers, and the story made new headlines in America and England. Soon Allen & Unwin arranged with another American publisher, Ballantine, to publish an authorized edition of Tolkien's books. Eventually, Ace Books promised it would not print any more copies of the books, and the whole matter was forgotten.

But, thanks to Ace's unauthorized edition, the works of J.R.R. Tolkien had received a great amount of publicity. Suddenly his name was a household word on both sides of the Atlantic. On campuses students formed Tolkien clubs. The hobbit Frodo Baggins, Bilbo's nephew, who is the hero in *The Lord of the Rings*, became a personal hero for millions of young people. In San Francisco, hippies talked about Frodo as if he were a real person. In New York City, the words "Frodo Lives!" were scrawled on walls. Tolkien's books were inspiring a whole generation.

For J.R.R. Tolkien himself, sitting in his modest little home with his wife Edith, the sudden popularity was a bit too much. He had always been a quiet, shy man, certainly not the type to enjoy being a celebrity. Now, though, there were television crews at the door asking for interviews, telephone calls from advertisers and companies eager to make money off of his work, and bags and bags of fan mail.

Tolkien responded to the popularity in his own way. He did not like to talk about himself, but he was happy to talk about his work. Of course, he was delighted that so many people found his stories enchanting. He had created the fantasy world of the tales because the modern world was a place that was too difficult and too unpleasant to remain in all the time. Now millions of readers around the world were reading his stories for the same reason. By diving into Tolkien's fantasies, people could forget for a while about the everyday world.

But Tolkien himself knew that the simple life in his tales was not reality. He had started writing *The Hobbit* with an impulse to return to the simple village of his youth. But he knew that things always change, and we cannot go back. Even at the end of *The Lord of the Rings*, Tolkien showed that the world of the story had changed. When the hobbits, weary from their long adventure, return to the Shire, they find life there has changed very much in their absence:

> "Many of the houses they had known were missing. Some seemed to have been burned down. The pleasant row of old hobbit-holes in the bank on the north side of the Pool were deserted, and their little gardens that used to run down right to the water's edge were rank with weeds. Worse, there was a whole line of the ugly new houses all along Pool Side, where the Hobbiton Road ran close to the bank. An avenue of trees had stood there. They were all gone. And looking with dismay up the road towards Bag End they saw a tall chimney of brick in the distance. It was pouring out black smoke into the evening air.

Not even in Tolkien's fantasy land would things remain the same, for in life, Tolkien knew, things continue to change until we die.

The saddest change in Tolkien's long life came in 1971, when his beloved Edith died at the age of eighty-two at a hospital near the home they had bought on the seashore.

Tolkien outlived his wife by two years. After her death, he moved back to Oxford. There, he received an honorary doctorate, the university's highest honor. That same year he was summoned to Buckingham Palace to receive the Cross of the British Empire from Queen Elizabeth. In the summer of 1973, a happy old man, he ventured to the seaside town of Bournemouth to stay with friends and soak up the sun. There, on September 2, he died. He had lived a full life, and had given pleasure to millions. He had never traveled much on the earth, but in his mind he had always been a traveler through the enchanted lands of his imagination. But in the end, he always knew, a traveler must come home, as Bilbo said in a poem he made after his adventures:

> Roads go ever on
> Under cloud and under star,
> Yet feet that wandering have gone
> turn at last to home afar.
> Eyes that fire and sword have seen
> and horror in the halls of stone
> Look at last on Meadows green
> and trees and hills they long have known.

A Selected Reading List

Books by J.R.R. Tolkien

The Hobbit
The Lord of the Rings Trilogy:
   The Fellowship of the Ring
   Two Towers
   The Return of the King
The Silmarillion

Books about Middle Earth

The Complete Guide to Middle Earth, by Robert Foster, Ballantine, 1985
The Tolkien Scrapbook, by Alida Becker, Running Press, 1979